Cute Pets Dress

Singing the Cute Pets song all time long

Authors / Images and Cover

Dirk L. Feiler

Tanja Feiler

The outfits

The girls working hard for making the second edition of outfits for the concerts of the Cute Pets. The new fashion design made by the girls of the

Cute Pets community: Angelina & Angela, Haeschen, Michelle and Kitty for image editing.

The newspaper making a interview and written an articel, publishing on the newspaper:

You rock

The Cute Pets are famous here in Petcity.

Musicians , authors and artists, designers , this is the Urbanization . Meanwhile, two members are married to members of Urbanization . They provide with its diverse art for the advancement of Petcity . Your latest song is daycare on the social project . We all look forward to the new album and concerts . The new album is almost finished . New concert tour ?

Through the newspaper article the Cute Pets belong almost to the celebrities. Therefore the images of the Cute Pets are everywhere.

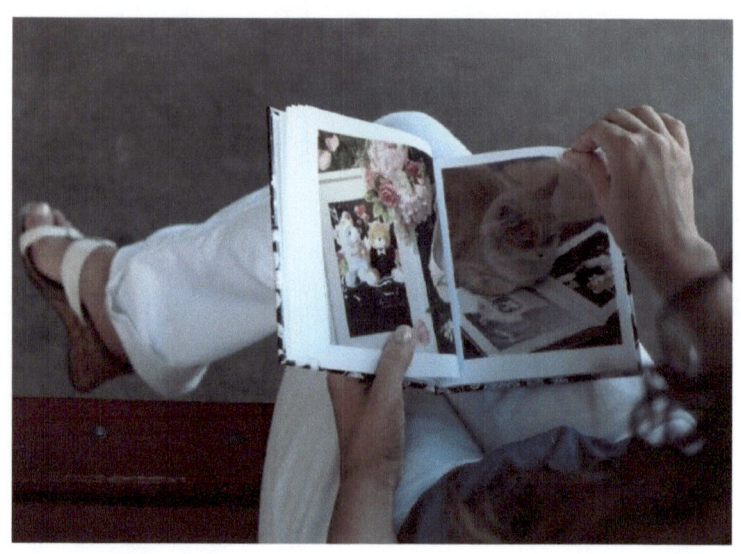

Sing the daycare song all time long